SPORTS HEROES AND LEGENDS

Shaquille O'Neal

Read all of the books in this exciting,
action-packed biography series!

Mia Hamm

Tony Hawk

Michael Jordan

Shaquille O'Neal

Jackie Robinson

Babe Ruth

SPORTS HEROES AND LEGENDS

Shaquille O'Neal

by Charlie Christian

BARNES
&NOBLE
BOOKS
NEW YORK

For Kieran and Nicole—great editors and true friends

Cover photograph:
© Mark J. Terrill/AP Photos

Contents

"Remember This Name"

Michael Jordan. Magic Johnson. Isaiah Thomas. Those were just a few of the NBA champion players who had been here before him. Shaquille O'Neal couldn't help thinking about that as he arrived at Kemper Arena in Kansas City, Missouri. He was actually playing in the 1989 McDonald's High School All-American game!

Since the first game in 1978 McDonald's had brought together the best players in high school basketball every year to face off on the court in an East versus West matchup. Players who dominated in this game had gone on to basketball stardom in college and in the NBA.

But did Shaquille really belong here? He believed he did, but he also knew everyone else wasn't so sure. Unlike other players at the 1989 game, including Kenny Anderson and Bobby Hurley, Shaq wasn't that well known to the basketball world yet.

Last year he had led his Cole High team in San Antonio, Texas, to a 35–1 season, and he was getting ready to top that record his senior year. It was enough to secure Shaquille a spot on Louisiana State University's roster, and Shaq had already signed a letter of intent to attend the college next fall. But since he had spent his first two years of high school on a military base in Germany, the hard work he'd done there to improve his skills hadn't really made an impression on many people back in America. Now he had to make up for lost time.

Shaquille was in the gym warming up for the game when he spotted a representative from Nike handing out free clothes and shoes to the star players. Excellent—he could use some new sneakers. But the rep had only brought stuff for the players he'd heard about, and Shaquille wasn't one of them. Shaq watched as everyone else got brand-new pairs of Air Jordans and fancy jackets. Finally he walked over and asked if there was anything for him. The rep dug around in his bag and came up with a pair of green Nikes Shaq describes in his autobiography as "raggedy."

Now Shaquille was just plain mad. Why was he being treated like this? He'd been invited here, right? It was time to show that Nike representative—and everyone else—why.

Taking a deep breath, Shaq headed over to Dick Vitale, the college basketball announcer on ESPN who was covering the McDonald's game. Vitale looked up at the towering player—

Shaquille was getting closer to seven feet every day—and waited to hear what he had to say.

"Mr. Vitale," Shaquille began, "remember this name: Shaquille O'Neal."

When the game got started, Shaquille was in it right away. In the opening minutes he blocked a shot and dribbled the ball all the way to the other end of the court. Just inside the free throw line he launched himself up for a massive dunk—which none of the three players guarding him could stop!

Immediately Dick Vitale started babbling, "Did you see that? Are you serious? Welcome to LSU, Shaquille O'Neal!"

Shaq didn't let up, scoring 18 points and grabbing 16 rebounds in the game. His awesome moves earned him the John Wooden MVP award, which he shared with Bobby Hurley. Air Jordan himself hadn't even been the MVP of the McDonald's All-American game he'd played in. Plus Shaquille's 16 rebounds tied him with several other players for third place in most rebounds scored ever in a McDonald's High School All-American game.

It was pretty amazing—after all the rough times Shaq had been through, he'd finally shown everyone what he could do. It hadn't been easy getting to that game in Kansas City, and Shaquille knew he still had lots of battles ahead. But he had a feeling he had some more excitement coming to him, too. And he couldn't wait!

Chapter One

A Giant Is Born

Most people think the basketball star who ended up reaching seven feet, one inch tall and weighing over 300 pounds must have been a huge baby—but when Shaq was born on March 6, 1972, in Newark, New Jersey, he was actually only seven pounds and eleven ounces.

Lucille O'Neal gave a lot of thought to the name she gave her first baby. She eventually chose Shaquille Rashaun O'Neal. "I wanted my children to have unique names," she explains. "To me, just having a name that means something makes you special." So what does Shaquille Rashaun mean? Little Warrior. "I was never little," Shaquille admits, "but I was always a warrior."

Shaquille's biological father was a man named Joe Toney, who had played basketball at Seton Hall University in New Jersey. Lucille and Joe never got married, so she decided her son should carry on her family's name of O'Neal. When Joe began to get involved with the wrong people, Lucille moved forward without him. She brought Shaquille to her mother's home, where she raised him for the first two years of his life.

Then Lucille met the love of her life, Philip Harrison. Philip knew Joe Toney from school, but Philip was taking his life in a very different direction. He asked Lucille to marry him, hoping he, Lucille, and Shaquille could all be a family. Phil even joined the army to be sure he could provide a good, stable life for his new wife and son. Later Lucille and Phil gave Shaquille some siblings—two sisters, Lateefah and Ayesha, and a brother, Jamal.

❝ We'd buy [Shaquille] pants on Saturday, and by the next Friday, they wouldn't fit. ❞
—Philip Harrison

When Shaquille was five, the family moved to Bayonne, New Jersey. "That's where my father really began disciplining me," Shaq recalls. Philip's hero was General Patton, who was famous for saying that his troops didn't have to love him, they just had to respect him. Someday they'd love him when they saw that his toughness had only been good for them. Looking back, that makes a lot of sense to Shaquille. He was always getting into trouble, and his dad came down pretty hard on him. "I got spanked every day," he shares. "[But] I had it coming."

5

Philip had lots of expectations for his son, and he made sure Shaquille followed his rules. Every morning he would walk into Shaq's room and try to bounce a quarter off his bed. If the quarter didn't bounce, Shaquille had to make his bed all over again!

But later Shaquille realized his dad was doing what he could to make sure Shaq didn't go down the wrong path. "If it hadn't been for Phil, I'm not sure what would have happened to me," he says. "I might be in jail now."

Since Shaquille was always tall for his age, he got teased a lot. Kids called him names like "Shaquilla the Gorilla" and "Sasquatch." By the time he was 11 years old, he was already six feet, four inches tall, so he had to stop trick-or-treating—people thought he was an older teen trying to scam candy on a kids' holiday. He was failing all of his classes in school because he was so down about being made fun of all the time, he stopped doing his work.

When Shaquille was still young enough to qualify for a discounted fare on the train, his mother had to bring his birth certificate with them on the ride to prove he really was his age!

The only thing Shaq could think to do was use his size to help him get revenge. "I became a bully," he says. "I learned how to fight." Every time word got back to his dad about another fight he'd been in, Shaquille had to face Philip Harrison's stern discipline. Shaq's pretty sure that's what helped him finally turn away from beating up other kids and focus on beating them in sports instead.

It was Phil who taught Shaquille how to play baseball, basketball, and football. "My dad used to throw me all kinds of passes [on the basketball court]," Shaquille relates. "He really taught me how to get a feel for the basketball."

❝I was one of those kids who thought they knew it all. My dad was trying to keep me off the streets, to keep me off drugs, trying to make me into somebody.... Luckily, I listened before it was too late.❞
—SHAQUILLE O'NEAL

Because Philip was in the army, he and his family had to move every few years to a new base. After leaving New Jersey for Fort Stewart, Georgia, Shaquille joined a youth football league. At the time it seemed like his best sport, and he won all three parts of a punt, pass, and kick competition. But people still bugged Shaquille about how big he was for his age. "Teams wanted to check his birth records to see if he was eligible," remembers Jimmy Martin, sports director of the youth activities program at Fort Stewart. And Shaq was actually one of the youngest players on his team!

Shaquille was focusing on football because he had an easier time with the sport than with baseball or basketball, but he really enjoyed basketball, too. The problem was, his legs were growing so fast that he was having trouble staying balanced and playing a smooth game on the court. His elementary school gym teacher at Fort Stewart, Henry Baker, remembers that Shaq was "easy to coach, but [not] that coordinated. He was large and his skill hadn't caught up to his size." Baker even felt that he'd seen other kids who were much more talented.

Shaquille also struggled with something called Osgood-Schlatter disease, another result of his enormous growth spurts. The disease affects the bones around the shins and knees, and during the roughest years Shaq had terrible pain in his knees and couldn't jump very high. "Even though I was six foot seven or six foot eight by the time I was fourteen, I couldn't dunk," he says. "I couldn't jump over a pencil." Shaquille had to take calcium pills and load up on certain foods to try and help with the symptoms until he got older and outgrew the problem.

But although his own body was making the game harder for him, Shaquille realized just how much he loved to play basketball. He knew all he needed was a coach who could help him get past his awkwardness and hit the right rhythm. Then his family made their biggest move yet—to a base in Wildflecken, Germany.

When Shaq was 13, his parents took him to a doctor, who predicted that he would grow to seven feet tall. Shaquille beat the prediction by an inch, maybe because he always had to go one better than what people said he could do.

At first Shaquille was upset. He'd never liked moving around because he felt like every time he finally made some friends, he just had to leave them. And now he had to start over in a whole different country! But Germany turned out to be better for Shaq than he ever imagined—mainly because of the people he met there.

First, there was Louisiana State University basketball coach Dale Brown. During the summer before Shaquille's sophomore year of high school, Brown ran a basketball clinic on the base where Shaquille and his family lived. Philip mentioned the clinic to his son and suggested he go ask the coach for help.

Shaquille went to the clinic and followed all the drills, but after the session ended, he stuck around to talk to Brown. He asked if Brown could give him an exercise plan that would help strengthen his long legs and give him the right body for basketball. Brown provided Shaq with some tips, then asked how long he'd been in the army. Confused, Shaquille explained that he was only 14.

Brown's jaw dropped, and the first thing out of his mouth was—"Where's your father? I want to meet your father right now."

Brown kept in touch with Shaquille after returning to Louisiana, and his encouragement and coaching advice gave Shaq the boost he needed to try out for the basketball team at his school, Fulda High.

Fulda's coach, Ford McMurtry, was impressed with Shaquille's height, but he'd seen plenty of tall kids who couldn't play basketball. When Shaq marched up to him at the beginning of his sophomore year at Fulda High and announced that he'd be the team's new center, McMurtry told him he'd have to earn the spot, no matter how tall he was. So Shaq pushed through the pain in his legs and worked as hard as he could to show his new coach he deserved to be center. And by the first official game of the season Shaquille was Fulda High's starting center!

Shaq scored 16 points in that game and also made it into double digits on rebounds. It was a great way to start off, but it wasn't enough for Shaquille. He decided to quit football altogether when he realized how easy it was to get a bad injury in the game. Instead he concentrated totally on basketball, working hard with Coach McMurtry and listening closely to all of the coach's advice on how to sharpen his game. "[Shaq] played hard in practice," McMurtry says. "When you taught him something, you could just see him soaking it up."

McMurtry was also one of the first people outside of Shaquille's family to get to know Shaq better and see what a good heart he has. Kids had always made Shaquille feel bad about being so big for his age, and he'd acted tough because that was what people expected of a big guy. But McMurtry insists that Shaq was "a gentle giant. . . . He was very engaging and never said a bad word about anyone."

That didn't mean Shaquille wasn't competitive when it came to basketball. He definitely wanted to win, and he'd do whatever he could to make it happen—on his team or even in pickup games on the army base. Shaq and his friend Mitch Riles used to go head to head all the time. They pretended to be their

Shaquille has always loved music as well as basketball. When he was a kid, he used to break dance in the hallways of his school. Once someone saw him and called the school nurse because it looked like he was having a seizure!

11

idols, Dr. J and Larry Bird. Unfortunately for Shaq, he had to admit that "Mitch was a lot closer to being Bird than I was to being Doc." But losing to Mitch just got Shaquille more fired up to take his game to a higher level.

The Fulda High School team was doing much better with Shaq than they had in recent years. Coach McMurtry remembers one play in particular, in a game against a team from Berlin. Most of the time players as big as Shaquille O'Neal are valuable on the basketball court because of the sheer force of their size—they can outreach opponents when it comes to dunking the ball, blocking shots, and grabbing rebounds. But every once in a while there's a big man in the game who can move like the smaller guys—who can dribble around defenders and twist and turn to get the job done. In the game against Berlin, Shaq showed for the first time that he might become one of those players. After an expert block he easily got control of the ball, then sent it down the court to a teammate for a clean layup. The Berlin team's coach was shocked, but McMurtry felt a burst of excitement—he could tell great things were in store for Shaq.

With Shaquille going strong, Fulda High's season went so well that the team even made it into the postseason play-off tournament. Coach McMurtry couldn't wait to see how far Shaq would take the team. Maybe they'd even snag the championship this time!

Then the coach got some bad news. Philip Harrison had been transferred again, back to the United States. The whole family had to pack up and return home right away, meaning Shaq would miss the play-offs.

The Fulda High squad won the last game Shaquille played with them, but no one could find Shaq afterward. Then Coach McMurtry discovered his star player in the bathroom, crying. Shaquille had really found a home on this team, and he was devastated about leaving before the end of the season. McMurtry gave Shaquille a hug good-bye, and then Shaq thanked the coach for everything he'd done for him. It was an emotional moment, and McMurtry wished Shaquille could stay. But he had a feeling big things were waiting for Shaq back in America.

Chapter | Two

Total Scrub

T he buzz started early—from the moment Shaquille O'Neal arrived at Cole High School in San Antonio, Texas, it was on everyone's minds. The school had its newest basketball star!

After his first meeting with Shaquille, Cole athletic director Joel Smith rushed into the office of Dave Madura, the basketball coach. "We've got ourselves a giant!" Smith announced, bursting with excitement. There was just one problem. "Where am I going to get shoes for this kid?"

Shaquille already wore a size-17 shoe—by the time he was a senior at Cole, he'd be up to a 20. In Germany he'd actually had to stuff his feet into shoes that were too tight for him, and Coach McMurtry remembers how eager Shaq always was to pull off the sneakers as soon as the team was on the bus.

But here at Cole High, Smith and Madura were going to do everything they could to give Shaquille what he needed

While Shaquille lived in Texas, there was a state rule against dunking in pregame warm-ups in high school games. But fans used to come to the games just to see Shaq dunk. Once an opposing team's coach instructed the referees not to come onto the court until the starting buzzer—because "these people all paid to see Shaquille O'Neal dunking in the warm-ups."

to bring their team all the way—including giving him shoes that fit right!

Since Shaq had transferred to Cole High too late in his sophomore year to start playing that season, Coach Madura decided to put him into a summer league to get ready for his junior year at Cole. Shaquille made the league's all-star team easily and impressed coach Louis Torres with his desire to improve.

"The best thing was that he was coachable," Torres shares. "He had a great attitude."

Coach Madura and his assistant coach, Herb More, were equally wowed by Shaquille's good nature and drive to work hard. "He had such a warm personality and a great smile," More says. "He also has a terrific sense of humor."

More had once been a player at Cole High himself, and at six feet, six inches tall, he was the only person who could really give

Shaq a good challenge during the team's practices. So More would play Shaq hard during practice, fouling him repeatedly since he knew that's what opponents would do. More wanted Shaquille to be ready for the worst that could come at him on court.

To inspire his son, Philip Harrison gave Shaq an old basketball from the gym he ran, telling him to "dream with it." Shaquille took the words to heart and actually slept with the ball every night, using it as a pillow!

More and Madura were happy to discover that Shaquille had already worked hard at being a complete player, not just a big guy who could swat the ball from someone's hands. "Shaquille was fully capable of getting a rebound and then dribbling the ball the length of the court," More says. "He could go all the way for a slam, throw a no-look pass, or pull up and take a 15-foot jumper." Shaquille was also finally able to dunk for the first time at Cole High, and once he got started, there was no stopping him!

Shaquille dedicated himself completely to basketball, making it the center of his world even when he wasn't on the court. At home he started watching all the NBA games broadcast on cable networks, studying the players' moves. He also found out as much as he could about the players themselves, learning why some talented guys made it and others never did.

Shaq listened in particular as the commentators talked about players who got banned from games because of using drugs. "I told myself that wasn't going to be me," he says. He'd already seen what drugs and alcohol could do to kids he'd known growing up, and this just gave him extra motivation to steer clear of the stuff. "There were kids doing drugs, even on the army base," he says, "but that wasn't for me."

Shaq knew he did have one bad habit, though—a temper. Everyone who knew him talked about what a fun, friendly guy he was. But Shaquille could also get angry fast when he thought someone was cheating him out of a point or win he and his team deserved or when someone tried to tell him he wasn't good enough. Of course, the anger could come in handy—as long as Shaquille used it the right way.

After witnessing an incredible play where Shaq caught a rebound in one hand, then brought the ball back up for a slam dunk, Cole High's opposing team's coach said the move was "NBA material or nothing is."

Before one game against a rival school, the opposing team's coach came over to Cole High's bench and promised his team would come out the winner. Shaq didn't hear the comment because he was busy warming up. But More made sure to tell him once he was done with warm-ups. "He just looked at me," More recalls. "Never said a word, but I got the message."

Shaquille played the team so hard that the force of his dunks slamming into the basket bent the rim *twice.* The teams had to play the whole second half with a bent rim!

With Shaquille getting better all the time, Cole High zoomed through the season undefeated—until they went up against Liberty Hill at the end of the year. Cole's record was 35–0 going into the game, and Shaq admits he was too cocky. He made some mistakes early, even getting called on a personal foul right on the opening tip.

Cole was trailing, but the team had hope. "We still could've won the game, but I missed two free throws with five seconds left and we lost," Shaquille recalls, still beating himself up for that moment. The loss stung even more because before the game, some of the Liberty Hill players had made racist remarks about Cole High's largely African American team.

Shaq came away with a lesson he knew he'd remember— games could come down to those couple of opportunities, and it was important that he never get too overconfident and give up the "killer mentality" that made teams win.

When Shaquille came back his senior year, he was ready to dominate anyone who challenged him, especially Liberty Hill. Showing he knew how to hold a grudge, he led Cole High to a massive victory over the rival school that season, making up for the year before. "We killed them so bad that their fathers could've been [the referees] and it wouldn't have made a difference," he says with pride in his first autobiography, *Shaq Attack*.

But Liberty Hill wasn't the only school being crushed by Shaq. As strong a player as he'd been his junior year, he was now turning into a force of nature. "It was absolutely amazing to see the difference," Liberty Hill's coach said. "Shaquille went through a physical metamorphosis from his junior to his senior year."

Shaq broke his coach Herb More's own Cole High scoring record when he notched 47 points in a game against Lampassas his senior year.

Now six feet, ten inches tall and 250 pounds, Shaquille definitely *looked* scarier than ever when he was facing down a player in front of the basket. But what made him even more

19

dangerous was that he was growing into his body, moving better on his long legs. "He is like a deer just learning to run," reported Clark Francis, editor of the recruiting magazine *Hoop Scoop.* "It is scary how good he could be if he continues to develop."

Cole High's offense now centered entirely on getting the ball to Shaquille and giving him space to take shots. He was averaging more than 30 points and 20 rebounds a game and often sat out for at least a full quarter after giving his team a gigantic lead.

People around the country were starting to hear about Shaq, especially after the way he'd played in the BCI tournament in Houston before the start of his senior season at Cole. The tournament gives top high school players a chance to show what they can do, and Shaq had been playing alongside future NBA talents like Kenny Anderson, Conrad McRae, and Allan Houston. Even in the midst of so many great players, Shaq had stood out. One game in particular got him attention—he was up against a kid who was being called the best center in the nation, Matt Wenstrom. Before the game Shaquille got into a fight with his dad, and that extra burst of anger pushed him on to destroy Wenstrom, dunking on him over and over again.

After that tournament letters started to come in from colleges showing interest in Shaquille. But Shaq had stayed in touch with Dale Brown ever since they met in Germany, and he was pretty sure he was headed to Louisiana State. He and his parents checked out the other schools, but in the end Shaquille signed the letter of intent for LSU.

Meanwhile Shaq still had an important task to take care of before graduating from Cole High—bringing the team a championship!

After an undefeated season the Cole High Cougars met Clarksville High in the state championship game, played in Austin, Texas, on March 11, 1989. "The thing I remember is the crowd," says Shaq's Cole High teammate Robert Dunn. "We looked up in the stands and couldn't believe how many people were there."

During Cole High's 1988–89 season, Coach Madura decided not to get a haircut until his team lost. Since they went undefeated all the way through the state championship game, his hair was pretty long when he finally cut it that spring.

The huge crowd wasn't the only reason Shaq felt extra motivated to win this match. Before the game Coach Madura had given his team an emotional speech in the locker room, asking them to win not only for themselves, but for all the other teams he'd coached. Deep down, Madura knew that since this was Shaquille's last year at Cole, it could also be Madura's last shot at nailing a championship—and he wanted it bad.

Shaquille couldn't stand the idea of letting his coach down. From the second the starting buzzer went off, he fought hard to control the game. The Cougars charged to a solid lead and held on to it until the fourth quarter. But Shaq picked up a few fouls, and Madura finally had to bench him because he was in danger of fouling out—giving Clarksville the perfect chance to steal the game away.

The Cole High Cougars averaged 80 points a game and beat most of their challengers by between 30 and 40 points during Shaquille's senior year.

With the game down to five minutes left, Clarksville brought the score to 54–53. Cole High had just one point on their opponents, and Madura knew he had to take the risk of sending his star back into the game. He'd hoped to wait a little longer, but it was now or never.

Shaquille knew exactly what he had to do. Once Coach Madura released him on Clarksville, Shaq exploded on the court. He helped his team finish the final minutes with a final score of 68–60. The Cole High Cougars were the Texas state champions!

Shaq had come a long way from the awkward teenager who couldn't jump and even the "kid from Texas" who'd blown people away at both the BCI tournament and McDonald's All-American game. His star was on the rise, and he couldn't wait to get to LSU and show the NCAA what he was really about.

Chapter | Three

Big Man on Campus

After Shaquille O'Neal became the one to watch his senior year of high school, he got calls from some big-name college coaches, including famous University of North Carolina Tar Heels coach Dean Smith. Smith even used his "big gun," former Tar Heel Michael Jordan, to try to lure Shaq to North Carolina.

A lot of the coaches who talked to Shaquille promised him everything he could ask for, most importantly a guaranteed position as a starting center for the team—even in his freshman year. But Dale Brown of LSU, who'd been in touch with Shaq for several years, told a different story. "Coach Brown said if I came to LSU and proved myself, I could be a starter. He put the emphasis on my proving myself."

Shaquille was up for the challenge, which was a good thing—because when he came to LSU and started playing with

Brown's team, he learned fast that the coach meant every word he'd said.

❝ We were quite fortunate to get a player and a person like Shaquille O'Neal to come to our school. He gave us so many great memories here at LSU. ❞
—DALE BROWN

There were already two star players on the squad—guard Chris Jackson and center Stanley Roberts, another "footer." A footer is someone at least seven feet tall, and Roberts was seven feet exactly. So the big question was, who was the better center, Roberts or Shaquille?

In the first few games of the 1989–90 season Roberts held on to his starting position and Shaq came in off the bench. Then after Shaquille led the team in rebounds with 17 in LSU's fourth game, Brown shifted the lineup to allow both Roberts and Shaquille to start, playing Roberts as a forward.

There was still a lot of talk about which of LSU's big guys had it in him to bring the team all the way. "I saw tremendous skills in both players," LSU assistant coach Craig Carse said. "Stanley was more skilled offensively, while Shaquille was a great athlete who could run, pull down rims, and played a hard, intimidating game."

Shaq's college dreams were almost sidelined when he only got a 680 on the SAT, but luckily his 15 on the ACT was high enough to qualify him for a basketball scholarship to LSU. Once he got there, he proved he deserved the chance, pulling in the highest grade point average of the entire basketball team—3.0!

Still, Shaq's game had some major problems. He was struggling with his free throws, and he got into foul trouble way too easily. During his freshman season he actually fouled out of nine of the LSU Tigers' 32 games.

Shaquille continued to work with Brown on getting past those obstacles, showing up to practices early and giving it everything he had. Brown was a real workhorse coach, who expected a lot from his players. If someone missed class, Brown insisted the player get up at five-thirty the next morning and run. But Shaq thrived under Brown's tough discipline because he was used to that attitude from his father. And he was as afraid of letting down Coach Brown as he was his own dad, so he devoted himself to improving his skills.

There were a couple of games where he really took off. Against Nevada–Las Vegas (who eventually became the national champions), Shaq poured in 17 points and grabbed 14 rebounds, helping LSU to a 107–105 victory. He had another great game against Loyola-Marymount, with 20 points, 24 rebounds, and a Southeastern Conference (SEC) record of 12 blocked shots. LSU took the game from Loyola-Marymount in overtime, with a final score of 148–141. Those 148 points were the most any team in the SEC had ever scored in a game!

Unfortunately, the LSU Tigers were defeated in the first round of the SEC play-offs and then eliminated in the NCAA tournament by Georgia Tech. But even though Shaquille's freshman year at LSU had its share of bumps and didn't end with a championship trophy, there was plenty to be proud of. He finished the season with an average of 13.9 points a game, and his average of 12 rebounds was the top in the SEC. He even shattered an SEC record for blocked shots in one season with an amazing 115.

During Shaquille's stellar sophomore year he set several LSU records. On December 20, 1990, he broke the single-game scoring record with 53 points against Arkansas State. His 25 games with double digits in scoring and rebounds made another record.

When Shaquille returned to LSU his sophomore year, the pressure was on big time. Chris Jackson had moved on to the

NBA, and Stanley Roberts had left the Tigers to play for a basketball team in Europe. He'd actually been disqualified from the team because of his poor academic performance, a reminder to Shaquille to take his classes seriously, which he always did.

Now that Shaq was the real leader of the team, Brown went out of his way to give his player all the help he could. He even invited former NBA champion centers Bill Walton and Kareem Abdul-Jabbar to come to Louisiana and work out with Shaquille. Shaq was thrilled to have two of his idols there at his side, giving him tips on how to stay out of foul trouble and shoot better.

❝No matter what you do, [Shaquille] can muscle you out of the lane. He just may be unguardable.**❞**

—GEORGIA COACH HUGH DURHAM

The lessons paid off, and even though LSU was ranked much lower than the previous season now that Jackson and Roberts were gone, Shaquille carried the team through some tough challenges.

It was a game in December that really made headlines. LSU was up against Arizona, the number two college team in the nation. Arizona's success was credited to what was being called the Tucson Skyline—the team's frontline trio of six-foot

28

eleven Sean Rooks, six-foot eleven Brian Williams, and seven-foot Ed Stokes. Could the LSU Tigers answer three big guys with just one, an 18-year-old sophomore?

If that sophomore was Shaq, then buckle your seat belts, sit back, and enjoy the ride!

Before the game, ESPN commentator Dick Vitale went to talk to Shaquille in the locker room. Vitale still remembered meeting Shaq at the McDonald's All-American game, and he knew this kid had it in him to blow people away. "Shaq, I don't think you can beat these guys," he told Shaquille. "But do your best."

Right then Shaquille decided that his best was good enough to give the Tigers a win and it was the perfect time to show the world. The game was televised across America, and tons of fans were tuned in to see the top Arizona team strut their stuff. But by the end of that game the name on everyone's lips wasn't a player from Arizona's squad—it was Shaquille O'Neal.

Shaquille was playing a decent but average game until the last few minutes. At that point he looked up and caught his mother's eye. She mouthed the words, "Take over," and Shaq listened. Suddenly he was everywhere on the court, dominating the game like he was the only guy actually playing. In just *six* minutes Shaquille scored an incredible 16 points!

Thanks to Shaq's superstar heroics, LSU squashed Arizona, 92–82. Including his last minute scoring, Shaquille had knocked in 29 points, grabbed 14 rebounds, and made six blocks and five steals. And he did all that in a total of just 28 minutes of playing time!

Suddenly all eyes were on Shaquille O'Neal, now being called the nation's best big man.

After his dazzling performance against Arizona in the 92–82 blowout, Shaquille did a dance for spectators that he called the "Shaq-de-Shaq." It was just the beginning of all the nicknames Shaq would later come up with for himself and his moves!

The Arizona game gave Shaquille the kind of national exposure he hadn't had yet, and everywhere he went, fans surrounded him. "You needed the entire police force, it seemed, to get Shaquille back to the bus after the games," marveled Kent Lowe, LSU associate sports information director.

Shaq loved the attention and tried to sign as many autographs as he could. He especially went out of his way for his younger fans since he knew what it was like to be a kid who looked up to someone. Even though Shaquille always insisted that athletes should never be true role models for children since that was the job of parents, he still knew that he was an idol to a lot of kids, and he took that seriously.

By the end of Shaquille's sophomore year there was no question he was the most exciting player in college basketball. He was the league's leading rebounder, with 14.7 per game, and he averaged nearly 27.6 points a game. He was chosen as Player of the Year by the Associated Press, *Sports Illustrated,* United Press International, and LA Gear. He was also awarded the Tanqueray World Amateur Athlete of the Year Award. "If people didn't know how great [Shaquille] was after his freshman year," Dale Brown says, "they certainly knew after his sophomore season."

In fact, Shaq's moves had made such a splash on the basketball scene that many people started to say he should leave LSU early and go out for the NBA. Experts assured Shaquille that it was almost a sure thing he'd go as the first pick in the draft. So why spend more time at LSU, risking an injury that could stop his NBA career before it had even begun?

Shaquille thought hard about what to do but in the end decided to stay in school for another year. It was very important to his parents that he get his degree, and it was important to him, too. He was hoping to stay at LSU for as long as he could.

It wasn't long into his junior year that Shaq started to wonder if he'd made the right choice. Defenders were playing him tougher than ever before—really pushing him and knocking him to the ground on a constant basis. "They'd beat [him up] all the time, and referees would actually tell him, 'You're big enough—quit crying about it,'" Dale Brown recalls.

As the season wore on, the beatings got more and more brutal, and Shaquille's anger and frustration built. Finally, during the 1992 SEC play-offs in Birmingham, Alabama, Shaq snapped.

The Tigers were playing the Tennessee Volunteers, and when Shaquille went up for a dunk, the Volunteers' Carlus Groves grabbed him and pulled him back from the basket. Similar flagrant fouls had happened to Shaquille so many times that season, and few of them were ever called. Shaq turned to Groves, furious, and took a swing at him.

Referees immediately surged forward to break the two players up, but the line had already been crossed, and within seconds both teams were up off the bench, running at each other. Dale Brown even lost his own temper, lunging at Groves and yelling at him for fouling Shaquille. "Players are like your sons after a while," Brown later said, explaining how he got so carried away. It was almost as hard for Brown to watch Shaquille take all the abuse as it was for Shaq to suffer it.

It was also hard for Shaquille's real father, Philip Harrison, to see what was happening to his son. Even though the previous year he'd convinced Shaq to stay at LSU and get his degree, now he realized it wasn't that simple.

Shaquille had finished his junior season with impressive

stats, this time racking up an amazing 157 blocks. He'd fought his hardest to help the Tigers advance in the NCAA tournament, but his 36 points and 12 rebounds hadn't been enough to keep LSU from being knocked out by Indiana in the second round. The season had been a mixture of highs and lows, but the lows were tipping the scale in Shaq's mind and in the minds of the people who cared most about him. He realized that college ball just wasn't fun anymore—not when he was always wondering if a career-ending injury was right around the corner.

Shaquille was so well known around Louisiana during his time at LSU that a couple living in Geismar, Louisiana, actually named their baby Shaquille O'Neal Long! When Shaq found out, he drove all the way to the Longs' home to meet them and take a picture with their new baby.

When he called a press conference in the gym of his old school, Cole High, in San Antonio, Texas, most people knew what to expect. The conference was held on April 1, but Shaquille promised reporters this was no April Fools' joke. It was for real—Shaq was coming out, making himself eligible for the NBA draft. So now the only question left was which team Shaquille would end up playing for.

Chapter Four

Center Stage

On June 24, 1992, Shaquille and his family were waiting eagerly in Portland, Oregon, for the NBA draft ceremony to begin. A month earlier the Orlando Magic had won the top pick in the draft lottery, and they'd made it clear who they were going to take with it—Shaquille was headed to Florida. But this was the night when it would become official. Any minute now David Stern, the NBA commissioner, would reveal which player was being chosen first.

Finally, just when Shaquille was about to burst from excitement, it happened—David Stern announced that the Orlando Magic had chosen Shaquille O'Neal as the first pick of the 1992 NBA draft!

Suddenly everything was happening so fast. Shaquille had chosen an agent, Leonard Armato, before the draft. Leonard had already gotten Shaq a great endorsement deal with Reebok

❝There were eleven guys sitting there with Shaq uniforms. So whoever came out of there with the winning ball was going to unveil their jersey.❞

—ORLANDO MAGIC PRESIDENT AND GENERAL MANAGER PAT WILLIAMS, ON ALL THE TEAMS HOPING FOR THE FIRST PICK IN THE 1992 DRAFT LOTTERY SO THEY COULD DRAFT SHAQUILLE

sneakers, and now he helped Shaquille work out a contract with the Orlando Magic that awarded him the largest rookie salary in the history of sports—$41 million for seven years. The Magic knew exactly what they had in Shaq, and they weren't about to let him slip away.

As exciting as the record-breaking salary was, Shaquille tried not to let the money go to his head. "I'm not about money," he insists. "I make more money in one year than my father made in his entire life, but that doesn't make me a better person than him." Shaquille was determined to work as hard as ever and to earn every penny of his paychecks. He knew he had a tough job ahead. The Magic had won only 21 games the previous season, losing the other 61. They were counting on Shaq to make the difference this year.

Fans in Orlando were already going crazy, thrilled to have Shaquille coming to their city and convinced he'd be able to do the trick. Ticket sales to Magic games were astronomical, and the Magic's management blasted the B-52's song "Love Shack" over their telephone lines. Meanwhile another "Magic" couldn't wait to see Shaq join the NBA—basketball superstar Earvin "Magic" Johnson. "Shaq will be great and I mean *great*," Magic promised.

Expectations were more than high—they were through the roof. With all the pressure, would Shaquille be able to come through in his first official NBA game?

It was time to find out on October 16, 1992. The Magic were up against their neighbors, the Miami Heat, in the first preseason exhibition game. Shaquille sat in the locker room before the game, his nerves out of control. He had only found out a few days earlier that the results of this game didn't count toward the overall season record, the way preseason games had in college. And even knowing that, he couldn't help thinking that how he played tonight would show both himself and everyone around him if he could really pull this off.

Twenty-five points, six rebounds, and three blocked shots later . . . things were looking good!

Shaquille continued to play well for the rest of the preseason, although it wasn't an easy ride for the Magic. Shaq was still adjusting to playing professional basketball, and his teammates were struggling to up the level of their own play.

Then before they knew it, it was time for the Magic's *real* first game of the season.

This time the Magic were facing off with the Miami Heat at home in Orlando. Shaq didn't score as many points as he had in their preseason matchup—this time he only had 12— but he did grab 18 rebounds, and most importantly, the Magic won the game, 110–100.

Shaquille was the first rookie in NBA history to be named Player of the Week in his first week in the league.

The team had begun the 1992–93 season with a victory over the team next door. Now it was time to take the show on the road!

The Magic were coming on strong, that was for sure. They won three of their first four games, and Shaq's numbers on points and rebounds were consistently in the double digits. The wins kept coming, and as November wound down, everyone could see that Shaquille's efforts to turn around his team were paying off. The Magic had an 8–3 record, and Shaq nabbed the NBA Player of the Month award. He was really doing it—he was proving he deserved all the faith Orlando had put in him!

Shaquille's dedication to Orlando didn't stop on the basketball court. As hard as he fought to win games for the Magic, he also did his best to give to the community he lived in. Remembering what it was like for many of the poor kids he'd grown up with in New Jersey, Shaq organized a huge meal on Thanksgiving called "Shaqsgiving." He wanted to feed every single homeless person in Orlando, no matter what it cost, and even spent the day personally helping to serve food to the over 300 people who came.

Before Thanksgiving was even over, Shaquille started thinking about Christmas. Orlando's newest benefactor returned for the December holiday, when "Shaq-a-Claus" gave out high-quality presents to tons of poor kids in the area. Shaq's old high school coach had called him a "gentle giant," and the title seemed to fit—Shaquille had a real heart of gold and a soft spot for people in need.

But the gentle giant was still a giant, and when he was on the basketball court, he played as fiercely as ever. The Magic had their ups and downs as the season went on, but there were

It took Shaq only 28 games to become the Magic's all-time leading shot blocker.

some exciting glimpses of what they could do when they were really on—like one game in particular on January 16, 1993, against Michael Jordan's Chicago Bulls.

66*He's doing it on raw talent now. I'd hate to see [Shaquille] when he learns how to play this game.*99

—THEN NEW YORK KNICKS PLAYER TONY CAMPBELL

The Bulls had won the NBA championship the past two years straight, and they were gunning for a three-peat that spring. But that night Shaquille gave Jordan and the rest of the Bulls a challenge they couldn't overcome, even on their own home turf in Chicago. Amazingly, Michael Jordan poured in 64 points, a high number even for His Airness himself. But *still* the Bulls couldn't answer the determination of Shaq and his teammates, and when the final buzzer sounded, the score was tied.

The game went into overtime, and the Magic kept fighting. At the end of the five-minute period they'd done it—they'd beaten the Bulls in Chicago, 128–124!

Shaquille had 29 points and a whopping 24 rebounds in the game, but it was more than just his stats. His energy and fire were rubbing off on his teammates, giving them the confidence they needed to take down a team like Jordan's champion Bulls.

Sometimes opposing teams weren't the only thing Shaq took down. *Twice* that season his dunks were so forceful that he actually broke the backboards, just barely getting out of the way as the structures collapsed. It happened first at the Phoenix Suns' arena, in a game on February 7. Only minutes into the game Shaquille's powerful slam dunk almost brought the basket down on top of him. The game had to be paused for 37 minutes while workers fixed the damage. Then at the end of the season Shaquille pulled a repeat performance in New Jersey against the Nets.

This guy was stronger than even *he* realized.

Fans were eating it up, swarming arenas and tuning in to Magic games on TV in huge numbers to see what Shaquille would do next. Shaq was so popular that when the 1993 All-Star game rolled around, he became just the fourteenth rookie in the history of basketball to be voted not only onto the All-Star team, but onto the starting lineup!

Shaq was thrilled, but not everyone was happy about him being the starting center for the East's squad. New York Knicks center Patrick Ewing had held that spot for the past three years straight, and he was generally looked at as the best center in the Eastern Division. Plus the Knicks coach, Pat Riley, had been chosen to coach the East in the All-Star game that year—and Pat didn't like having to see his star player start the game on the bench!

66When you're seven feet tall, you're supposed to have some limitations, but with Shaq, I just haven't seen any.99
—THEN NEW JERSEY NETS CENTER SAM BOWIE

But the fans had voted Shaq above Ewing for a reason. Going into the All-Star break, Shaquille's stats were higher than Ewing's. Shaquille was second in the league for rebounding, second in blocked shots, second in field goal percentage, and seventh in scoring. "If I was a fan, I'd want to come and see Shaq play, too," Shaquille told reporters with a sly smile.

Even though the fans were clamoring for Shaq, Pat Riley was careful to give Shaquille and Ewing equal minutes on the court for the All-Star game. But Shaquille made his minutes count, scoring 13 points in just 14 minutes of playing time in the first half. Shaquille did his best to ignore the controversy reporters were building over his having "stolen" Ewing's starting spot and just enjoy the whole All-Star experience. He was especially proud to be able to give his All-Star ring to his father, a way of saying thanks for everything Phil had done for him.

But Shaquille was already eyeing another ring—the NBA championship ring. Once the All-Star break was over, it was back to business. Shaq was doing everything he could to see the Magic make the play-offs that year, but it was a tough battle. Sometimes the pressure really got to him, and he finally snapped during a game against the Detroit Pistons on March 30.

The two teams came to the game hungry. "We were both fighting for a play-off spot and it showed," Shaquille later wrote in *Shaq Attack*. The rivalry was especially intense for Shaquille because he was up against Detroit's center, Bill Laimbeer, who was known for playing a hard, physical—even dirty—game. Shaq had often objected to the way Laimbeer played him, and this game in particular he felt Laimbeer was smothering him every time he touched the ball. With just two minutes left in the game Shaquille received a pass and then felt Laimbeer surround him in what he later described as a "bear hug."

That was it for Shaq. As soon as Laimbeer let go, Shaquille went after him, angry and demanding to know what Laimbeer's problem was. Then Laimbeer's teammate Alvin Robertson ran in and grabbed Shaq, worried he was going to hit Laimbeer. Robertson hung on, not letting go, and yelled at Shaquille. Shaq couldn't believe the refs weren't doing anything. When moments passed and Robertson still wouldn't get out of his face, Shaquille felt all of his frustration come to the surface, and in one furious moment he threw a punch at Robertson.

Shaq was immediately ejected from the game, suspended from playing in the Magic's next game, and fined $10,250. He explained later that he'd just been tired of getting fouled so hard, claiming he would never commit a foul that he knew could cause serious injury to the other player. Still, he knew he shouldn't have let his temper get the best of him. He'd learned years ago that it wasn't the right way to solve a problem.

Shaq's 1993 rookie year All-Star jersey went for $55,000 in a charity auction held over the All-Star weekend, while Michael Jordan's sold for only $25,000!

So for the rest of the season he tried to keep himself under control, focusing on the goal of making the play-offs. Unfortunately, the Magic just barely missed out on the last available slot in the Eastern Division, which went to the Indiana Pacers.

But Shaquille had a lot to be proud of. The Orlando Magic's record had improved by 20 wins in just his first season with the team. His stats were high across the board, and he was named NBA Rookie of the Year shortly after the end of the regular season. "I'm very proud and happy to win this," he said. "It's been a long year, but I learned a lot and I'm already looking forward to next season."

So were the fans in Orlando—because they had a feeling Shaquille was just warming up!

Chapter Five

Making Magic

One of the reasons Shaquille was so popular with fans was that he didn't just play the game well, he put on a real show for spectators. So it wasn't long before Hollywood came calling—Shaquille was actually asked to do a screen test for a movie, *Blue Chips*, before the 1993 All-Star break.

Blue Chips starred Nick Nolte as a basketball coach who gets a little too caught up in the pressures of winning. (That was something Shaquille could understand!) The movie's director, William Friedkin, wanted real basketball players to take the parts of Nolte's players so the basketball scenes would feel real. Friedkin was happy with Shaquille's audition, so once the deal was worked out, Shaq was all set to spend the summer after his rookie year filming his first major motion picture!

Shaquille had a great time making the movie and even convinced the director to make some small changes in the plot and dialogue. Plus there was an unexpected bonus from making *Blue Chips*—Shaq got to know a future teammate, Anfernee "Penny" Hardaway.

Hardaway was another talented basketball player who'd been asked to act in the movie, and right around the time filming began, he was drafted by the Orlando Magic. So at the same time that he and Shaquille were working on *Blue Chips,* they were also developing a chemistry together for the upcoming Magic season. They both knew that everyone's hopes were on the two of them to form a new dynamic duo that would take the Magic all the way.

66*Once you start talking to [Shaquille], you realize that there's a real person who is caring and committed and wants to be a part of the community.*99

—Orlando mayor Glenda Hood

As the 1993–94 season got going, something was definitely working. The Magic seemed to be getting better all the time, and they were clearly contenders for a play-off spot this time around. "[The Magic's management] have surrounded Shaq with better players," observed NBC commentator Peter Vecsey. Vecsey was quick to point out that Shaquille was still the key to

Orlando's strength, but everyone knew that one great player couldn't win games alone.

Once again in 1994 Shaquille was voted onto the All-Star team as the starting center for the East, above Knicks star Patrick Ewing. And by the end of the season the Magic were nipping at the heels of the powerful Knicks, coming in right behind New York for second place in the entire Eastern Division. More exciting for Shaquille, the Magic had made the play-offs!

They were up against the Indiana Pacers, the team who had beaten them out for a play-off spot the previous year. Shaq fought hard, but Indiana's coach Larry Brown had his players triple-team the Magic's go-to guy, and the strategy eventually worked—Indiana eliminated Orlando in three games.

The loss was disappointing, but Shaquille knew that his team had come a step farther this year, and all they had to do was play even better next season.

Shaquille didn't give himself much of a break from basketball that summer, joining the U.S. national team (called "Dream Team II") for the 1994 World Basketball Championships. Following in the footsteps of the original Dream Team's incredible performance at the 1992 Olympics, the U.S. team dominated the tournament, beating their challengers by an average of 37.8 points. Dream Team II faced Russia in the gold medal game, crushing them 137–91. Shaquille was a big reason for the national team's success, and he was named the MVP of the tournament.

It was an exciting summer, but as it came to an end, Shaq had just one thing on his mind—this year he was determined to help the Magic win an NBA championship. He knew he was finally surrounded by players who could really make it happen. Along with Penny Hardaway, the Magic had Nick Anderson and Dennis Scott, both solid supporting players. Also, the team had brought in Horace Grant from the Chicago Bulls, where Grant had won three championships alongside Michael Jordan.

Here's a little-known fact about Shaq—he's totally superstitious! If he has a really good game, he'll be sure to imitate whatever he did before that game in the future. One of his routines? A pregame meal of pizza and spaghetti!

Shaquille's gut instinct that this year would be his season turned out to be right. The Magic zoomed through the regular season, finishing with a record of 57–25, the top in the Eastern Conference. And Shaq's scoring average of 29.3 put him ahead of the rest of the league.

The Magic were back in the play-offs, and this time Shaquille wasn't going to let anyone knock them out!

They were up against Boston in the first round. It was the last year the Celtics would play in the Boston Garden, so the team had extra motivation to go for a championship win. But they were no match for Shaquille's Magic—Boston fell to Orlando in four games.

Shaquille had done it—he'd taken his team farther than they'd been before, to the Eastern Conference semifinals. Now he just had to keep on going, all the way to the finals. But first he had to defeat a team that had dominated the entire league for three years in a row, led by a player called the greatest to ever play in the NBA—Michael Jordan.

Jordan had recently returned from his first retirement, and in his short time back with the Bulls he'd jump-started his former teammates and helped them grab win after win, securing the Bulls' spot in the play-offs. Not only were the Bulls regaining their rhythm on the court, but with Jordan back they had that extra mental edge of intimidation. Who could top Michael Jordan, the unbeatable?

Shaq was ready to prove that if anyone could, it was him.

Game one took place in Orlando, and the Magic came on strong. Shaquille led his team in scoring and rebounds, sinking 26 points and grabbing 12 rebounds. He even made 12 of his 16 free throws, an impressive number for Shaq since he still struggled at the line.

Nick Anderson also came through for the Magic, playing tight defense on Jordan and allowing him only 19 points. Horace Grant, eager for a chance to prove himself against his former teammates, contributed some solid plays, as did Penny Hardaway. Together the Magic showed they had become a real team, and when the buzzer sounded, they had the game, 94–91.

It was a great way to start the series, but Shaquille tried not to get overconfident. He knew Jordan had a history of coming back bigger than ever after a loss. And that's exactly what happened in game two, when Michael scored a massive 38 points to help the Bulls to their victory.

Now it was off to Chicago for game three. Could the Magic take Michael Jordan's Bulls on their home court? It was time to find out.

Jordan did everything he could to make the answer a no, racking up 31 points in the first half of the game. But Shaquille showed Jordan he'd met his match, scoring 28 points of his own along with his 10 rebounds. "He is a real Superman and I am a real Superboy," Shaq said. And the game went to Superboy, as the Magic pulled out a 110–101 win.

Unfortunately, beating Michael in Chicago went to Shaquille's head, and he fell down on the job in game four. Foul trouble limited his playing time, and he made only 17 points and turned the ball over to the Bulls five times. Even with the strong shooting of Shaq's teammate Dennis Scott, Orlando lost the game 106–95.

Uh-oh—it was time to shape up, and fast.

Shaquille knew he couldn't afford to let the Bulls get a third win because once they were on top, nothing would stop them from sealing the deal and winning the whole series. Shaq rallied his teammates to fight with everything they had in game five.

Shaquille led the charge, pouring in 20 points on offense. But he also came through where it really counted—on defense. The Bulls just couldn't get their score up with Shaq constantly blocking a shot or nabbing a rebound. In the end Orlando whipped the Bulls, 103–95.

Now the Magic were just one game away from the Eastern Conference finals. But it would be one of the toughest games they'd ever faced.

❝When Shaq backs into you, it's like a house falling on you.**❞**

—MIAMI HEAT CENTER RONY SEIKALY

Chicago was playing hard—the Bulls weren't ready to start their summer break yet. They controlled most of game six, and it didn't look good for the Magic when the Bulls scored a three pointer to open up an eight-point lead with three and a half minutes left on the clock.

But amazingly Orlando managed to stay calm, even though they were in the hole to a team led by superstar Michael Jordan himself. The Magic fought back, scoring 14 points in the remaining minutes. After contributing 25 points in the game Shaquille added on a final slam dunk to give the Magic their last couple of points, bringing the final score to 108–102.

Shaquille could hardly believe it. His team had just become the first since 1990 to eliminate a Michael Jordan–led Bulls squad from the play-offs! He'd just defeated a three-time NBA champion team, with a star player who'd begun to seem untouchable.

It was an amazing high for Shaq—the biggest moment of his NBA career so far. But he couldn't relax yet because now the Magic were moving on to the Eastern Conference finals, where they were meeting another old rival—the Indiana Pacers.

The Magic started off on a good note, winning the first two games of the series at home in Orlando. But Indiana did just as well on *their* home court, where they picked up games three and four.

It was back to Florida for game five. This time Shaquille took over. He racked up an amazing 35 points and 13 rebounds, daring the Pacers to get in his way. Indiana did their best, but in the end they couldn't catch up to Shaq, and the Magic won, 108–106.

For game six the Pacers looked to their play-off hero, Reggie Miller. Miller was known for his ability to make clutch shots and sink three pointers when games—and series—were on the line. He didn't let his team down, scoring 20 points in the first quarter to give Indiana an early lead of 31–20. It was downhill from there for the Magic. Miller was determined to own the game, and his final total of 36 points helped Indiana to its crushing defeat of Orlando, 123–96.

Ouch—Shaquille had just seen his team get massacred.

One thing was for sure—he wasn't going to let it happen again. Game seven was all about Shaq and the Magic's defense, shutting Reggie Miller down and making sure Orlando came out on top. This time the Pacers learned what it felt like to be trounced as the Magic finished with a massive victory of 105–81.

The Magic were going to the NBA finals.

In 1996, 24-year-old Shaquille was the youngest player selected as one of the 50 greatest NBA players of all time.

Chapter | Six

A New Hometown

A s excited as Shaquille was for his first appearance in the NBA finals, he knew he faced some tough competition. The Magic were up against the Houston Rockets, who held the 1994 NBA championship title and were far from ready to let go. Shaquille would be matched up with the Rockets' star center, Hakeem Olajuwon—a player so talented, he'd been chosen before Michael Jordan in the NBA draft!

Shaquille had always admired Olajuwon and had even asked him for advice over the years. But now Shaq's job was to do whatever he could to knock his idol off the pedestal and steal the championship title away.

Game one was played at home in Orlando, and the boisterous cheers from fans were music to Shaq's ears. Inspired by all the support, the Magic zoomed ahead to a 20-point lead in the second quarter. Shaquille was sure his team had this game—

in fact, he knew in his gut that they were going to win the whole series. He was *on*—nothing and no one could stop him.

And that's when things went wrong.

"To this day, I regret that in my first finals, I didn't treat my opponent as an equal," Shaquille later shared.

The Magic had let their strong season and early lead in the game go to their heads, and the Rockets took advantage of this weakness. By the end of the third quarter Houston had not only caught up to the Magic, but whizzed right by them, building their own seven-point lead.

Both teams fought hard in the fourth quarter, pushing the game into overtime. But when the Magic missed some key opportunities, the Rockets managed to walk away with a 120–118 victory.

Orlando's confidence was shaken, and Houston went on to win the next three games for a 4–0 sweep of the finals. Shaquille's average of 28 points per game was something to be proud of, but Olajuwon reminded Shaq who was boss, averaging 32.8 points and 11 rebounds across the series.

The loss was a crushing disappointment for Shaquille, but he didn't give up hope. "I'm going to get [to the finals] again before I retire," he promised, already thinking about next year.

Unfortunately, Shaquille was forced to miss the first 22 games of the 1995–96 season after breaking his thumb in a preseason match. He was incredibly frustrated watching the games from the bench but tried to relax and enjoy his forced vacation from playing. When a reporter asked what he was up to, he joked he was spending his time "eating steak, going to movies, waking up and not doing anything."

Meanwhile the Magic were going strong without him, cruising toward a record of 17–5. Shaquille was happy to see that his teammate Penny Hardaway was really hitting his stride on the court, leading Orlando to win after win in Shaq's absence. But he wasn't so happy when people started saying that his return might *hurt* the team instead of help them since they'd been doing surprisingly well without him.

Shaq put the question to rest after his first game back, against the Utah Jazz. He scored 26 points and grabbed 11 rebounds, opening the game with a classic rebound-dunk that knocked the basket support loose. After the game Orlando's Horace Grant explained that his team had adjusted to playing without Shaquille and done a great job of it but that they were

---

66 *People try to limit me, but I would never limit myself. I could never do just one thing, especially if I have the opportunity to do more.* 99
—Shaquille O'Neal

56

still stronger with him than without him. "It's a little bit like when you're reading and you think the light's fine, and then somebody comes along and turns on a big, bright lamp," Grant explained.

With Shaquille back in the lineup, the Magic went on to finish with the second-best record in the Eastern Conference, behind the Michael Jordan–led Chicago Bulls. Their 60 wins and 22 losses made the season the best ever for an Orlando Magic squad. And even after having to readjust to the game after his injury, Shaquille still finished third in the league in scoring, averaging 26.6 points a game.

The Magic barreled through their first play-off opponents, the Detroit Pistons, knocking them out in three straight games. The Atlanta Hawks put up more of a fight, blocking Orlando's efforts for a second sweep with a win in the fourth game of the series. But after game five they were out, and the Magic were moving on to the Eastern Conference finals.

It was like last year's semifinals all over again—the Magic were facing off with the Chicago Bulls. Shaquille was convinced

---

The Magic's 1996 first-round play-off sweep of Detroit was the first time the Orlando Magic had ever swept a series.

things would go the same way they had before, and even after losing the first game of the series, he told reporters he wasn't worried, explaining, "It's only one game."

But Michael Jordan had played the full season, and with expert defender Dennis Rodman added to the Bulls lineup, the team was once again unbeatable. This time it was the Magic who felt the sting of being swept as they saw their dreams of returning to the NBA finals crushed by the powerful Bulls.

Shaquille was disappointed, but he didn't have much time to sit around being sad because he was in for one of the most exciting summers of his life. First there was the 1996 summer Olympics, held in Atlanta, Georgia. Playing for Dream Team III was a real thrill for Shaq, especially since it gave him the chance to go for an Olympic gold medal in his own home country. To no one's surprise, the Americans dominated the tournament, and soon enough the gold medal was theirs after a 96–69 win over Yugoslavia.

But the real high point of Shaq's summer came in August, when his first child was born. Shaquille's girlfriend at the time, Arnetta Yarbourgh, actually went into labor right before the opening ceremony of the Olympics. Shaquille was at her side when their daughter, Taahirah, was born, because family always comes first for Shaq. "The happiest I felt was the day my daughter was born," Shaquille later said. "She's beautiful."

Shaq's senior yearbook photo.

Shaq with actor Nick Nolte on the set of Shaq's first film, *Blue Chips.*

Shooting over Hakeem Olajuwon in the 1996 All-Star game.

Taking on Michael Jordan in the Eastern Conference finals in 1996.

Making a dunk for the U.S. team at the 1996 Summer Olympic Games in Atlanta.

At the 1997 opening of a Planet Hollywood restaurant in Hong Kong, Shaq performs one of his raps.

Celebrating the Lakers' 2000 NBA championship win.

Shaq hands out
presents to schoolkids
in Los Angeles during
the 2001 holiday season.

In January 2002,
President Bush
congratulates a
towering Shaq for
the Lakers' 2001 NBA
championship title.

Fans cheer as Shaq goes past in the 2002 Lakers' victory parade celebrating their third consecutive NBA championship.

On top of his new role as a father, Shaquille faced another major life change the summer of 1996. While training for the Olympics, he signed a deal to leave the Magic and join the Los Angeles Lakers out in California.

❝ *When you combine the size and strength [Shaquille] has, it makes him an almost unstoppable force.* ❞

—LAKERS VICE PRESIDENT JERRY WEST

As Shaquille explains, several factors contributed to his decision to leave Orlando. He'd always loved the Lakers, and it was a childhood dream come true to have the chance to play on their legendary squad. He also felt that the Magic's administration was no longer giving him enough respect for what he brought to the team. The Lakers, however, went all out to recruit Shaq—they had to do a lot of fancy footwork, reorganizing their team in order to afford the hefty contract they finally offered Shaquille, paying him almost $121 million over seven years.

Another big reason Shaquille decided to move out west was that over the past few years he'd been building a solid entertainment career outside of basketball. "Right after [the Magic's] seasons ended, I used to fly out to Hollywood and make movies," he recalls. "I'd been going to L.A. the last four summers, so I already had a house on the beach."

Shaquille had followed up *Blue Chips* with roles in the feature films *Kazaam* and *Steel*. He'd also lived out his dream of recording rap music. *Shaq Diesel* was released in 1993, and *Shaq Fu: Da Return* came out in 1994. So a move to Los Angeles meant Shaq would be able to play basketball in the same city where he had all the connections for his work in music and film, making his life a lot easier.

Shaquille volunteers for a project called "Read a Book for Mom" that encourages kids between the ages of seven and 18 to read more. The winner of the project's annual contest gets tickets to watch Shaq play, and the winner's mother gets free flowers for a year!

Unfortunately, Shaquille's first season with the Lakers was *not* very easy. Even though it started well, with Shaq nabbing the NBA Player of the Month award in December, a knee injury in February caused him to miss 28 games. For the second time he was stuck spending a major part of an NBA season on the bench!

At least he was back in time for the postseason—ready to take the Lakers all the way.

The Lakers faced the Portland Trailblazers in the first round of the 1997 play-offs. Shaquille came in strong, proving his time away hadn't put a dent in his power on the court. In game one he scored a whopping 46 points, beating his own play-off high record. With Shaq on fire, the Lakers squashed the Blazers, 95–77.

After three more games the Lakers had won the series, and it was time to take on the Utah Jazz in the Western Conference semifinals.

The Jazz picked up games one and two, but the Lakers came back in game three with a resounding 104–84 victory. Then game four went to the Jazz, despite Shaquille's 34 points and 11 rebounds. Suddenly game five was do-or-die for Los Angeles. One more loss, and they would be eliminated.

Shaquille, who'd been making solid contributions the whole series, poured in 23 points and another 11 rebounds but fouled out of the game with almost 12 minutes left on the clock. The Lakers faltered with their star center on the bench, and the team fell to Utah 98–93.

Yet another painful disappointment—how many would Shaq have to face? He was hungry for a championship ring, and every year he missed out just made him want it even more.

Shaquille couldn't help wondering if the Lakers would ever earn an NBA title, the way things were going with the squad.

"We had no chemistry," he later said, "a bunch of me-me-me guys and a couple of coaches who had trouble getting respect."

Shaquille was especially worried about one of his teammates, Kobe Bryant. Bryant had been drafted by the NBA right out of high school the previous summer, so in Shaq's eyes he was still a kid during the frustrating 1996–97 season when they first played together.

66[Los Angeles] is a great city. . . . Even though I'm 26, I'm still a kid. Here, it's like being a kid in a candy store.99

—SHAQUILLE O'NEAL

Amazingly, Shaquille had actually met Kobe when he really *was* still a kid, back when Shaq was playing for the Orlando Magic. After a game at home in Orlando, "I walked into the locker room and met this young high school kid who everybody was saying was gonna be a great player," Shaquille remembers. The kid's favorite player was Penny Hardaway, and Shaq watched as Hardaway took a quick picture with him, scribbled an autograph, then hurried off.

Shaquille felt bad, so he walked over and spent more time with the high schooler, who explained that his dad had been in the NBA and he hoped to be one day, too. Shaq swears that after that meeting, he was sure it would happen. Of course, what he didn't know was how soon or that he and that kid would be forming a one-two punch for one of the most famous teams in NBA history!

And now here they were, teammates on the Los Angeles Lakers. Kobe, whose father, Joe "Jellybean" Bryant, had played eight seasons in the NBA, was just 17 years old when he played in his first NBA game. And even though Shaquille remembered having a gut feeling about that kid in the locker room, he still felt like Kobe wasn't quite ready for all the responsibility. After Shaq fouled out of the crucial game five against Utah in the play-offs, it had been left to Kobe to keep the Lakers alive—and he hadn't been able to do it.

So the big question was—would Shaq and Kobe and the rest of the Lakers be able to pull themselves together next year to come out on top?

Chapter Seven

Purple Reign

Shaquille had high hopes for the 1997–98 season, and he was especially proud when his teammates chose him as their captain before the season began. He knew all the Lakers needed to do was find a way to work together, and then they'd be unstoppable.

Shaq helped his team get off to a strong start but was sidelined by yet another injury in November—this time a bad abdominal strain. Shaquille was in a lot of pain, and it didn't help that he had to sit out for 20 games, missing the entire month of December.

Even scarier, the doctors warned Shaquille that if the tissue in his abdomen didn't heal right, his career could be over. "For a while, I wasn't sure I was going to beat the injury," Shaq remembers. "I was scared I would never be able to play basketball like I once did."

When it came time to suit up again, in January, Shaquille was more than a little nervous. Could he still be the "Shaq Attack" fans were so psyched to welcome back?

It didn't take long to answer that question—and to Shaquille's relief, the answer was a big fat yes!

❝I want to be the best, and I will be the best, and I'm not going to let anybody stop me.❞
—SHAQUILLE O'NEAL

Shaquille was such an awesome force on the court in his first games back that he was actually named Player of the Month for January, averaging 29 points and 12.8 rebounds per game. When February rolled around, Shaq was once again playing in the All-Star game. He'd faced down a painful and dangerous injury and come out on top. But would he finally have the championship trophy to show for it this year?

The Lakers finished the regular season with a solid record of 61–21 and took down their opponents in the first and second rounds of the play-offs. But when they reached the Western Conference finals, they were forced to battle last year's rivals, the Utah Jazz. And the Jazz did it again, knocking out the Lakers and crushing Shaq's dream of an NBA title.

The following season was cut short by a players' strike that didn't get worked out until the winter, and the Lakers never really got a good rhythm going. They were swept in the play-offs by the San Antonio Spurs, and Shaquille was given a rough time in the press by reporters who pointed out that teams Shaq had played on had been swept in five of the previous seven years.

Some people said the problem was that Shaquille was too distracted by all his other projects. His latest rap album, *Respect,* was released that year, along with a book of fairy tales he'd written called *Shaq and the Beanstalk and Other Very Tall Tales.* How could he lead his team to a championship when he had so much going on outside of basketball?

But Shaquille insisted that when he was on the court, his focus was 100 percent on the game. He even argued that his other careers helped him be a better basketball player, especially his passion for music. "Music makes you dance, and in order to dance, and dance properly, you have to have rhythm," he said. "I have rhythm on the court." He went on to explain that this was the key to his ability to make moves only the smaller guys could usually do, something he was known for.

In Shaq's mind, the reason the Lakers kept coming up short was clear—they needed a coach who could make them a real team, not just a group of talented guys who didn't know how to work together. Sort of like what Phil Jackson had done for the

Bulls, who had suffered through seven years without a championship even with Michael Jordan leading them until Jackson came along and helped them grab the prize.

In fact, maybe the Lakers didn't just need someone *like* Phil Jackson. Maybe they needed Phil himself!

Shaquille started talking to the Lakers management about trying to lure Jackson back into the NBA. Coach Jackson had retired in 1998 after taking the Bulls to their sixth NBA championship in eight years, and at first he didn't seem all that interested in coming back. But when the Lakers went after him full force, he finally decided to go for it.

 On February 10, 1998, Shaq scored his 10,000th career point.

Shaquille was thrilled. Deep down, he was sure that with Phil Jackson in charge, he would finally get to wear a championship ring.

Shaq was so excited to get to know his new coach that when the tour for his latest rap album took him to Montana over the summer of 1999, he decided to stop by Jackson's cabin there. It was a surprise visit, and Shaq didn't know what to expect. But the last thing he thought was that his new coach's first assignment for him would be to help him move a tree!

When Shaquille and his bodyguard Jerome first arrived at Jackson's house, Phil wasn't even home. So Shaq hung out with Jackson's wife and two kids, jumping on their trampoline and going for a swim in the nearby lake. Then Phil got back from his bike ride and saw Shaquille in the water.

"You see that tree?" Phil said, pointing to a dead tree that had floated onto his property and sat in the yard. "Move it."

Together Phil, Shaquille, and Jerome tied a rope around the tree and dragged it off the property and into the lake. Shaquille was pretty confused at first, but then he realized something, thinking, "This man is challenging me, just like my dad when he threw me [into the pool] . . . and taught me how to swim."

Shaquille's scoring average of 28.3 points per game in the 1997–98 season was the highest of any Laker since 1970.

It was a great way to start the relationship because Shaquille had endless respect for his father, and now he had the same respect for the new Phil in his life—the coach he hoped would take him and the rest of his team all the way. From there the bond between the two of them only grew until Shaquille was calling Jackson his "White Father."

Now the question was, would the other players respect Jackson as much as Shaquille did? Enough to help them finally band together and win a championship?

When the 1999–2000 season started, it was Kobe Bryant, not Shaq, who had to sit out from an injury. But Jackson helped the team play well without Bryant, and the Lakers were 12–3 when Kobe rejoined the squad.

As talented as Kobe was, Shaquille couldn't help being a little worried about what his return would do to the team. They'd been doing okay without him, and maybe they'd start having the same old problems now.

But Shaq's fears were soon put to rest when he saw the way Jackson brought Kobe back in. Phil was known for his emphasis on an offensive strategy called the triangle, which he'd used with the Bulls to take the pressure off Michael Jordan and spread around the scoring responsibility. Now he was coaching the Lakers on the same thing, teaching them how to share and work in the best interests of the team, not just try to put on a one-man show.

Amazingly, the Lakers were catching on very fast. They won 20 of their first 21 games with Bryant back, and midway through January they had an incredible 31–5 record. Finally

Shaquille seemed to have gotten past his curse of injuries—he was healthier than ever. He missed only one game during the first half of the season, and that was because of a suspension from getting into a fight with a player from another team.

The Lakers were cruising along with a 16-game winning streak when they got a harsh wakeup call from the Indiana Pacers on January 14. The Pacers ended the streak with a 111–102 defeat. A lot of people were calling the Pacers the best team in the East that year, and Shaquille realized that if he made it to the NBA finals, he might just be meeting the Pacers. But there was still plenty of time to make sure if that happened, a different team would come out the winner!

Unfortunately, the loss to the Pacers had punched a hole in the Lakers' confidence, and they lost six of their next nine games. With their record down to 34–11, they were losing the top spot in the Western Conference to the Portland Trailblazers. Jackson did his best to fire his team up again, and they notched some wins before the All-Star break and then came on strong afterward.

Meanwhile Shaquille dominated the All-Star game, scoring 22 points and grabbing nine rebounds. He was named co-MVP of the game, sharing the award with fellow big man Tim Duncan. It was Shaq's first MVP in the NBA, and it meant a lot. But not as much as his dream of an NBA championship title.

—SHAQUILLE O'NEAL

On February 29, 2000, the Lakers met the Blazers on their home turf in Portland. The teams were tied with records of 45–11, and they'd both been sizzling in recent games. Shaquille walked into the Rose Garden that night telling himself that this was the biggest game of the regular season for the Lakers. If they won here tonight, they would go all the way. "I was on a mission," he later shared.

After many white-knuckled moments of trading the lead back and forth, the Lakers came out on top when it mattered, taking the game with a final score of 90–87.

Yes!

It was just the boost the team needed. Jackson reminded his players to keep their focus, not let up until they'd pulled out even farther ahead of the Blazers. And soon enough the Lakers had zoomed through a 19-game winning streak, beating their 16-game streak from earlier in the season.

But the most exciting game for Shaquille came on March 6, his birthday. Shaq came into the game feeling on top of the world. He was having the best basketball season ever, and the rest of his life couldn't be better. Shaquille and Arnetta, the mother of his daughter Taahirah, had broken up, but they remained friends, and Shaquille saw Taahirah all the time. Shaquille had since met and fallen for Shaunie Nelson, and on January 11, Shaunie had given birth to his son, Shareef. Shaq was thrilled to be a father twice over, and his new baby boy gave him one more reason to show the world what he could do.

The Lakers were playing the Clippers that night at Staples Center, the new arena that was actually home to both Los Angeles teams. Shaquille was excited for the birthday party he was throwing himself after the game, and at first he wasn't giving his all on the court. Then Coach Jackson gave him a tough reminder that he was there to play, and his uncle joked that it would be pretty cool for Shaq to score 50 points on his birthday.

Hmmm . . . that would be cool, wouldn't it? Well, maybe he should go for it!

Suddenly Shaq was on fire. He had 42 points by the end of the third quarter. The fourth quarter got started, and fans were going crazy as Shaquille made shot after shot. He zoomed right by the 50-point mark, finishing with an incredible career-high 61 points.

Happy birthday, Shaq!

Everything Shaquille had dreamed of was happening. The Lakers were playing awesome basketball, and when the regular season ended, their 67–15 record was the best in the entire league. Now it was time for the postseason, when Shaq's biggest dream would be on the line—would his team finally be the last ones standing in the NBA championship?

 Shaq's cars have to be specially designed for him—their interiors are pulled out and then the seats are moved back 10 inches so he can fit inside!

Chapter Eight

Staying on Top

Before the Lakers could fight for a championship, they had to get through the play-offs—something they hadn't been able to do since Shaquille had joined the team in 1996.

But everything was different this year, right?

The Lakers cruised through the first two games against the Sacramento Kings, their first-round play-off opponents. Game two was a total blowout, with a final score of 113–89. The wins went to Shaquille's head, proving him right that he didn't have to worry about anything.

Only that wasn't exactly true. Because games three and four were on Sacramento's home turf, and suddenly things were going the other way. The Kings took game three, 99–91. Then game four was a natural disaster for the Lakers—Sacramento devastated them 101–88.

Uh-oh.

Now Shaq was getting nervous. After the incredible season his team had just finished, were they really about to go down in the first round of the play-offs?

The two Phils in Shaquille's life—his dad and his coach—did their best to get him pumped up again. They reminded him that he never played well in Sacramento and that the deciding game five would be back home in Los Angeles. So Shaq tried hard to listen up and told himself that if his father and Coach Jackson weren't freaking out, he shouldn't, either.

What he *should* be doing, he knew, was getting ready to play some amazing basketball. And that's just what he did in game five, pouring in 32 points and grabbing 18 rebounds to help the Lakers to another rout, this time 113–86.

Phew—the series was theirs!

Shaq was riding high from the triumphant turnaround when he heard the news he'd barely let himself hope for all season—he'd been named the league's MVP! He'd had a huge year on the court, leading the league in scoring with an average of 29.7 points per game and coming in second place for rebounds and third for blocked shots. He even had a career-high average of assists, 3.8 per game, showing how Coach Jackson's efforts to teach his top players to share had really paid off. Shaquille knew he'd finally deserved the award this year, and it just made him prouder than ever of all of the season's accomplishments.

Now it was time for the Western Conference semifinals, where the Lakers would face the Phoenix Suns. Shaquille kept his confidence in check—he knew the Suns had some talented players who could give him and his team a run for their money. Playing smart, the Lakers won the first three games of the series. Even after a bad loss to Phoenix in game four, Shaq stayed calm, and the Lakers came back in game five to grab the win and the series.

The Portland Trailblazers were already waiting to take the Lakers on in the Western Conference finals. They had a team with some serious depth—players like Scottie Pippen, who had won six championships alongside Michael Jordan and with Coach Jackson; Rasheed Wallace, a real powerhouse; and seven-foot-three center Arvydas Sabonis.

But the Lakers had home court advantage, thanks to a stronger season and that all-important win over Portland back in February. So game one was at the Staples Center in Los Angeles, and Shaq was on fire. His 41 points and 11 rebounds gave the Lakers a 109–94 victory.

The Blazers came back in game two, out for blood. They soon got it, destroying the Lakers 106–77. Now the Lakers had to play the next two games of the series in Portland. They rose to the challenge, winning both games to give themselves a 3–1 advantage in the series. One more win and they were on to the finals.

Shaq received 120 of 121 possible first-place votes for the 1999–2000 regular season MVP award, making him the winner by a bigger margin than any player before him—including Michael Jordan!

But Portland wasn't making it easy. The Blazers left everything on the floor, coming away with games five and six to tie the series at three games apiece. The Western Conference title was up for grabs. "You either win and keep going," Phil Jackson told his players, "or lose and go home."

With everything on the line the Lakers proved once and for all that they were a different team this year. Even after going down 16 points in the third quarter, they didn't give up. It was truly a team effort that brought them back, but Shaquille was leading the charge. He scored half of his 18 points in the fourth quarter, even making eight of 12 free throw attempts, the one skill he still struggled with. "I've never felt higher on a basketball court in my life," he later said.

When the final buzzer sounded, the Lakers were ahead 89–84. They were going to the NBA finals!

Early predictions turned out to be true—for the championship title, the Lakers would be fighting the Indiana Pacers, the team that had knocked them down from a winning streak during the regular season. Did the Lakers have it in them to come out on top this time?

Only three other players in the NBA played more minutes than Shaquille during the 1999–2000 season.

They sure did in game one, which quickly turned into a blowout as Los Angeles sent the Pacers home with a crushing 104–87 defeat. Game two had a scary moment as Kobe Bryant had to be helped off the floor after a bad fall. But Shaquille and his teammates picked up the slack, with Shaq turning in 40 points, and the Lakers held on for a 102–96 victory. Unfortunately, they couldn't do it again in game three, which Kobe sat out to rest his sprained ankle—Indiana had their first win of the series.

Kobe was back in game four, and it showed. The two teams stayed neck and neck until the final seconds, pushing the game into overtime with a tie at 104 points. Early into overtime Shaq fouled out of the game, and at first he was scared it would cost his team a victory. But Kobe reassured him that he would take care of it, and he did—the Lakers pulled off a 120–118 win. It was especially meaningful for Shaquille to see how Kobe had grown as a player—they were trusting each other on the court in a way they never had before.

The Lakers were feeling good, seeing that championship trophy in front of their eyes . . . until game five, when the Pacers handed them a painful 120–87 defeat, their worst loss of the season.

It was time to get down to business.

Game six was at the Staples Center, and all Shaq wanted was to give his fans a championship party. The Lakers had done it 116 points later, beating Indiana's 111 points and giving Shaquille his first ever NBA championship win!

"Purple-and-gold confetti started coming out of the ceiling," Shaquille remembers. "Fireworks exploding, people rushing the court like a concert." It was a beautiful sight for him, and he started to cry from sheer relief at having finally proved all the doubters wrong. Soon enough he was holding both the NBA trophy and the finals MVP trophy, and he was overwhelmed with emotion. He'd shown everyone that he could bring a team all the way.

"Everything I ever wanted in basketball was right there in front of me on June 19, 2000," he later wrote in his second book, *Shaq Talks Back,* "the night I had been waiting for since I first picked up a ball as a five-year-old in Newark, New Jersey."

Shaquille O'Neal was a champion.

Of course, as amazing as that moment was, it didn't last forever. And pretty soon it was time to get ready for the 2000–2001 season, when Shaq faced a new pressure—*staying on top.*

❝*Give the credit to the big guy.***❞**

—KOBE BRYANT, REFERRING TO SHAQ, THE NIGHT OF THE
LAKERS' 2000 CHAMPIONSHIP WIN

Once a team snags a championship, they become the team to beat. Every other team in the league is out to take them down so they can say they beat the champions. As frustrating as all those years without an NBA title were for Shaq, being an underdog clawing his way up was different from this new position of guarding the top spot.

One smart move the Lakers made before the start of the new season was acquiring power forward Horace Grant, who had played with Shaquille in Orlando. Shaq actually helped convince the Lakers management to go after Grant, certain he'd help round out the team. Now, Shaquille was sure, his team would be unbeatable again this season.

Los Angeles opened the 2000–2001 season on October 31,

playing—of all teams—the good old Portland Trailblazers. Even on Portland's home court at the Rose Garden the Lakers managed a 96–86 win, boosting their confidence even higher. They were definitely unstoppable.

Or were they?

The next night the Lakers were back at home at the Staples Center, where they received their championship rings in a special pregame ceremony. But their opponents that night, the Utah Jazz, stole the game away, 97–92.

From there, things went downhill. The Lakers continued losing games, and Shaq just wasn't playing at his best. On November 30 the Lakers scored only 88 points to match the Seattle Supersonics' 121, making the game one of the team's worst losses since Shaquille had become a Laker.

The trust Shaquille had been feeling with Kobe Bryant last season was starting to fade as Bryant began to ignore Coach Jackson's lessons about sharing the offense and instead tried to do it all himself.

❝ *You can't have two Batmans. You have to have one Batman and one Robin.* **❞**

—HORACE GRANT, ON THE SHAQ-KOBE
CONFLICT DURING THE 2000–2001 SEASON

Frustrated, Shaquille felt his own performance slip on the court. His problem with shooting free throws was worse than ever as competing teams went all out with the "Hack-a-Shaq" defense. Basically this involved fouling Shaquille over and over again whenever he had the ball because the chances of him getting a basket on his own were way too good, but the chances of him making a foul shot were slim.

Shaquille started working with a coach who'd tried to help him on his free throws back in college, Ed Palubinskas. Palubinskas kept Shaq around after every Lakers practice, trying to get his percentage up, but it didn't seem to be helping.

Suddenly the highs of only months ago were giving way to terrible lows for Shaq. The fans waiting to greet his team were there for Kobe, not for him, and his young teammate's jersey was outselling his two to one. Bryant wasn't playing good team ball, but he *was* pulling off some amazing plays, earning Player of the Month awards and rave reviews from sports commentators. Shaquille, on the other hand, was seeing his stats drop way down. Coach Jackson even criticized Shaq in the press, saying he wasn't giving the game his all that season.

The Lakers really hit bottom in early January, when their fellow Los Angeles team, the Clippers, served them a crushing loss, beating them by a massive 23 points. The world champion Lakers were ranked far above the Clippers, and there was just no way to explain a loss like that—except for the fact that the Lakers were in deep trouble.

By the All-Star game in February, the tension between Shaquille and Kobe was still high, and Shaq even asked to have his locker moved away from Bryant's.

This was bad—really bad. Could Shaq and Kobe find a way to work together again in time to help the Lakers hold on to their championship title in the spring?

Chapter Nine

Three-peat!

After the 2001 All-Star break, the Lakers knew it was do-or-die. Shaquille and Kobe had to find a way to get over their problems with each other and play the kind of ball they'd played the year before if they wanted to repeat as champions.

Amazingly, it started to look like that just might happen.

In a game against the Charlotte Hornets, Kobe and Shaq *both* shone. Kobe nabbed the second triple double of his career (getting into the double digits for scoring, assists, and rebounds), and Shaq looked like his old self with 38 points and 12 rebounds.

Meanwhile Shaquille's work with Palubinskas was finally paying off—his free throw percentage was on the rise, climbing steadily from a dismal 37.2 to a respectable 56.4. When other teams noticed this, they stopped using the Hack-a-Shaq so much, and Kobe was a little looser about passing the ball.

It was especially satisfying for Shaq to show off his new abilities on the free throw line against the Dallas Mavericks, whose coach, Don Nelson, was often credited for creating the Hack-a-Shaq defensive strategy. During the Lakers' matchup against the Mavericks, Shaquille's 29 points included an impressive 11 of 15 free throw attempts. After adding in 11 rebounds and five blocked shots, Shaq easily helped Los Angeles to a 119–109 win.

By the second week of March the Lakers had fought their way back to first place in their division. But they couldn't hold on for long, and the spring was a tough one as they seesawed back and forth between triumphant victories and frustrating losses.

It was down to the final games of the regular season, and the Lakers were riding a good wave. Their second-to-last game was against the Portland Trailblazers, who had defeated them

Shaquille has a Superman *S* tattooed on his arm—it's a running theme for Shaq. The Superman logo is engraved in the headlights of one of his cars, and he has tons of framed Superman comic book covers in his house. Whenever he slams a hard dunk at the Staples Center, they play the *Superman* theme song over the loudspeakers!

twice that year after the Lakers' opening win of the season. Shaquille knew that coming out on top in this game would be crucial to the confidence level he and his teammates would need going into the play-offs. Could they get the win they needed?

Both teams showed up ready to fight, and the players' passions were close to the surface. At one point Blazers teammates Arvydas Sabonis and Rasheed Wallace even had a brief scuffle with *each other*. Later Sabonis hit Kobe Bryant in the face while Bryant was going up for a shot. Shaquille immediately approached Sabonis and warned, "You can do that to your teammate, but not to mine," showing the developing bond between himself and Bryant.

Whatever had changed between the players, it was working—after Shaq broke a tense 99–99 tie between the teams with a sleek jump shot, the Lakers went on to win 105–100.

The team's final regular season game, against the Denver Nuggets, also went their way, with Shaquille making every one of his 13 free throws. The Lakers were now the Pacific Division champions and ready to go to the play-offs!

Their first-round challengers were none other than the Portland Trailblazers, but this time the Lakers were ready for them. Shaquille had the time of his life as he and his teammates swept their rivals in three games, thanks in large part to Shaq's new abilities at the free throw line.

Shaquille missed a Lakers game on December 15, 2000, for a very important reason—so he could attend his graduation ceremony at Louisiana State University, where he'd finally made up all of the remaining credits after leaving school early to enter the NBA. "It means a lot to be a college graduate," he said proudly, also joking that LSU now stands for "Love Shaq University"!

Next it was on to face the Sacramento Kings in the second round. Games one and two belonged to Shaq. After scoring 44 points and pulling down a whopping 21 rebounds in the first game, Shaquille "slipped" to just 43 points and 20 rebounds in the second. He was red-hot!

Sadly, Shaquille received some tragic news before game three—his cousin, a firefighter in New Jersey, had died on the job. Shaquille was understandably upset and wasn't sure he'd be able to play, but he knew his cousin was no quitter, and he wouldn't want Shaq to quit, either. Shaquille did his best to keep control over his emotions as the Lakers took the game, 103–81.

It was time to get the broom out after game four—the Lakers had swept another play-off series! This time it was Kobe Bryant who'd stepped up, scoring 48 points. After the victory

Shaquille gave Bryant a hug and told him what a great job he'd done. Finally the two of them were in sync with each other.

❝ *It's like being married. We need each other.* **❞**

—SHAQUILLE O'NEAL, ON HIS RELATIONSHIP

WITH KOBE BRYANT

If there was any doubt about the genuine warmth that had grown between the two players, that was put to rest after Kobe's 45 points helped the Lakers take down the Spurs in the first game of the 2001 Western Conference finals. Shaquille came over to Kobe in the locker room after the game and told him, "You're my idol," meaning every word. He was so happy with how things had changed between them, both on and off the court.

The Spurs put up a fight in game two, and the Lakers' final 88–81 victory didn't come easily. But games three and four were total routs, with the Lakers winning by 39 and then 29 points.

Unbelievable—the Los Angeles Lakers had just swept the *entire* play-offs!

Now if they could just win four more straight games, they would have a record-breaking unbeaten postseason. But the Philadelphia 76ers, winners of the Eastern Conference title, had something to say about that.

The Sixers were tough opponents. Their star, Allen Iverson, had snagged the MVP award for the regular season—the smallest player ever to hold the title, at six feet and 165 pounds. Iverson's teammate Dikembe Mutombo was Defensive Player of the Year, and the Sixers had the best record in the league for the 2000–2001 season. The team's coach, Larry Brown, had even won Coach of the Year!

Of course, going up against the player who'd taken away his MVP award only made Shaq hungrier for a championship win. And since Kobe Bryant was originally from Philadelphia, a victory against his hometown team had extra meaning for him as well.

Game one was intense, and the teams traded the lead back and forth, pushing the game into overtime. Together Shaq and Kobe did their best to keep the Lakers on top during overtime, but in the end Philadelphia pulled off a 107–103 win. Kobe's performance during regulation time hadn't been his strongest, and he resolved to shape up before the next game.

The Lakers had lost their chance for an undefeated postseason, but they sure hadn't lost the championship yet—and they weren't about to!

Los Angeles came back in game two, walking away with the victory after another tight game. Game three was the same story, with a final score of 96–91. The Lakers led the series 2–1, but

Along with all of his other generous charity work (including the annual Shaqsgiving and Shaq-a-Claus events), Shaquille has granted 12 wishes for the Make-A-Wish Foundation, an organization that helps terminally ill children see their wishes come true.

Philadelphia had been in every game. What Los Angeles needed was a decisive win, one that would crush the Sixers' spirits.

They got just that in game four, beating Philadelphia 100–86. Now a second consecutive championship was just one win away. Shaq could taste it . . . but could he bring it home?

Oh yeah, baby, he could!

Shaquille did it all in game five—29 points, 13 rebounds, and five blocked shots—to help the Lakers to a 103–93 victory. The Lakers were once again the NBA champions, and Shaq was awarded his second-straight finals MVP trophy!

"I've never seen a better player in my life," Coach Brown said in tribute to Shaquille.

This year's win was even more precious than last year's in some ways because it hadn't come easily. After a long and troubled regular season the Lakers had come back to not only reclaim their NBA title, but do it in spectacular fashion, winning 15 out of

16 postseason games. Even though they'd narrowly missed going undefeated, their performance was still a new play-off record.

So, could they do it . . . *again?*

Two in a row was great, but already Shaquille was dreaming about a third. Unfortunately, before the start of the 2001–2002 season, Shaquille had surgery on his left pinkie toe, and even after healing from the operation he continued to have trouble with the toe—as well as with his right big toe—throughout the year. The ongoing pain was probably partly to blame for some of the problems he had on the court that fall.

Shaquille's eight blocked shots in game two of the 2001 NBA finals tied a record set in the play-offs by legendary centers Bill Walton and Hakeem Olajuwon.

The Lakers were having a better year than the previous season but still not matching what they'd done in 1999–2000. During a game against the Chicago Bulls, Shaquille actually got so upset after being bumped by Bulls player Brad Miller that he hit Miller, landing himself a three-game suspension and a $15,000 fine. Shaq's temper had cooled off a lot over the years, and Coach Jackson was worried that this wasn't a good sign.

But Shaquille got himself back under control, receiving a special reminder of what really mattered in life that winter with the birth of his second daughter, Amirah. Shaquille was now living with Shaunie Nelson, the mother of Amirah as well as their son, Shareef, and his growing family helped him keep his focus.

Despite their occasional rough spots the Lakers made it to the end of the season with a solid record of 58–24, second place in the league.

Just like last year, the Lakers were facing the Portland Trailblazers in the first round of the play-offs. And history repeated itself as Los Angeles swept the Blazers in three games.

Another old rival, the San Antonio Spurs, waited for the Lakers in the Western Conference semifinal matchup. The Spurs kept the Lakers from another sweep, winning one game of the series, but Los Angeles still took the series 4–1.

The Sacramento Kings were next, and they put up a tougher fight, stretching the series all the way to seven games. But the Lakers came through when it mattered, beating the Kings in game seven 112–106. Shaquille's new skills at the free throw line were crucial to the victory—he made 11 out of 15 foul shots!

Many fans were surprised to see the New Jersey Nets emerge the winners from the Eastern Conference finals, meaning they would move on to face the Lakers in the 2002 NBA finals. The Nets had some strong players, including star point guard Jason Kidd, but this was the first time in history the team had made it to the finals.

Shaquille knew overconfidence could cost him, but he was pretty sure his team had what it took to defeat the Nets. Just to be safe, he still went all out in the series, averaging 36.3 points and 12.3 rebounds a game. And it turned out he only had to do it for four games because the Lakers pulled off an amazing sweep of the finals! It was the first NBA finals sweep since Houston had swept Shaquille's Orlando Magic team in 1995, and Shaq felt great being on the other end this time.

He'd done it—he'd taken the Lakers to their third NBA championship in a row!

Coach Jackson told the press that it was more than just Shaquille's talent on the court that had given them the wins— it was also his ability to really lead the team and keep calm

---

66From this day on, I would like to be known as the Big Aristotle, because it was Aristotle who said, 'Excellence is not a singular act but a habit.' **99**

—SHAQUILLE O'NEAL, AFTER WINNING THE
2001 NBA CHAMPIONSHIP

---

under pressure. During game three the Nets had surged to a seven-point lead with just under seven minutes left, and it was Shaq who stayed cool and gave his teammates the encouragement they needed to get back on top. "It's at those times that Shaquille becomes the most influential player in the game," Jackson related.

The icing on the cake came in the form of a third-straight NBA finals MVP award, a statement about the kind of player Shaquille had grown into. The young boy who'd once been "awkward" on his too long legs was a distant memory and so was the rookie star who often let his anger and frustration get the best of him. With three NBA championships behind him and the hopes of more to come, Shaq had truly become a basketball superstar.

 Shaquille is the only player besides Michael Jordan to be named MVP of the NBA finals three years in a row!

Living the Fairy Tale

Shaquille started the 2002–2003 year with another surgery, this time on his right foot. He was forced to sit out the beginning of the season but came back on November 22 to help the Lakers defeat the Chicago Bulls, 86–73. In his 21 minutes of playing time Shaq scored 17 points and grabbed seven rebounds. Not bad—but Shaquille still said he felt a little rusty. He promised fans he'd be giving them what they wanted soon enough—more big plays and big wins and then, come spring, another NBA championship!

Shaquille is under contract with the Los Angeles Lakers through the 2005–2006 season, but he's already started to think about what he'll do after he retires from basketball.

First on his list is finally tying the knot with Shaunie Nelson. Shaquille lives with Nelson and his four children, Taahirah (Shaq's daughter with his former girlfriend Arnetta), Myles (Shaunie's son from a previous relationship, whom Shaq considers his own), and Shaquille and Shaunie's son and daughter, Shareef and Amirah. "I want to [get married] when I can focus on nothing but my marriage," Shaquille says, explaining why the wedding plans are on hold until his retirement from basketball.

Shaq's other dream may come as a surprise to some people—he's planning on a career in law enforcement!

Shaquille has many family members in the field, and he's actually already an honorary deputy for the Orange County sheriff's office in Orlando, where he lives during the NBA's off-season.

Making the world a better place to live in has deep, personal meaning for Shaquille because he grew up seeing what it's like not to have very much, and he knows all too well the dangerous paths that can lead kids down. It's why he's excited at the idea of becoming a police officer or sheriff, and it's also why he's continued to give both time and money in generous amounts to charities over the years—especially to his number one organization, the Boys and Girls Club.

"I know this life is a fairy tale," Shaquille says of his amazing time in the NBA. And for someone who admits to being a little kid who's never really grown up ("he's one of the nicest kids I've ever been around," Jerry West once joked), a fairy-tale life is just fine—but he's not about to forget the people out there who aren't as lucky as he's been.

For now Shaq will keep playing the game he loves with everything he's got, but with so many exciting things to look forward to, he can accept that someday his professional basketball career will come to an end.

He's determined to leave the sport on a high note instead of playing until he can no longer dominate the game. And unlike many players, who move into other aspects of basketball through becoming coaches, general managers, or commentators, Shaquille intends to walk away completely.

"I'm gonna leave the game, and I'm gonna watch the game and hope that the younger generation will make the game better, like we made the game better," he says.

Shaq knows there are kids out there waiting to follow in his footsteps . . . but it's a good bet his size 22 EEE shoes will be tough to fill.

CAREER STATS

Season	Team	Games	Rebounds	Assists	Steals	Blocks	Points	Season scoring average
1992–93	Orl.	81	1,122	152	60	286	1,893	23.4
1993–94	Orl.	81	1,072	195	76	231	2,377	29.3
1994–95	Orl.	79	901	214	73	192	2,315	29.3
1995–96	Orl.	54	596	155	34	115	1,434	26.6
1996–97	LA-L	51	640	159	46	147	1,336	26.2
1997–98	LA-L	60	681	142	39	144	1,699	28.3
1998–99	LA-L	49	525	114	36	82	1,289	26.3
1999–00	LA-L	79	1,078	299	36	239	2,344	29.7
2000–01	LA-L	74	940	277	47	204	2,125	28.7
2001–02	LA-L	67	715	200	41	137	1,822	27.2

AWARDS

First player to lead SEC in scoring, rebounding, field goal percentage, and blocked shots in the same year, 1991

SEC Athlete of the Year, 1991

SEC Player of the Year, 1991, 1992

NBA Rookie of the Year, 1993

Gold medalist, 1994 World Championship of Basketball

Gold medalist, 1996 Olympics

All-NBA First Team, 1998, 2000, 2001, 2002

All-Star Team, 1993, 1994, 1995, 1996, 1997, 1998, 2000, 2001, 2002

Named one of the 50 all-time greatest NBA basketball players, 1996

NBA MVP, 2000

All-Star MVP, 2000

Finals MVP, 2000, 2001, 2002

BIBLIOGRAPHY

Books

Gutman, Bill. *Shaquille O'Neal: A Biography.* New York: Pocket Books, 1998.

Gutman, Bill. *Shaquille O'Neal: Basketball Sensation.* Brookfield, Conn.: Millbrook Press, 1994.

Kaye, Elizabeth. *Ain't No Tomorrow: Kobe, Shaq, and the Making of a Lakers Dynasty.* New York: McGraw-Hill, 2002.

O'Neal, Shaquille. *Shaq Talks Back.* New York: St. Martin's Press, 2001.

O'Neal, Shaquille, with Jack McCallum. *Shaq Attack!* New York: Hyperion, 1993.

Rappoport, Ken. *Shaquille O'Neal.* New York: Walker Publishing Company, Inc., 1994.

Schaefer, A. R. *Shaquille O'Neal.* Mankato, Minn.: Capstone Press, 2003.

Smith, Pohla, and Steve Wilson. *Shaquille O'Neal: Superhero at Center.* New York: Sports Illustrated for Kids Books, 2003.

Sullivan, Michael J. *Sports Great Shaquille O'Neal.* Berkeley Heights, N.J.: Enslow Publishers, 1998.

Newspaper and Magazine Articles

Chappell, Kevin. "Has Shaq Gone Hollywood?" *Ebony,* December 1998.

McCallum, Jack. "The Shaq Factor." *Sports Illustrated,* June 17, 2002: p. 32.

Mead, Rebecca. "A Man-Child in Lotusland." *The New Yorker,* May 20, 2002: pp. 48–67.

". . . Shaq Facts." *Sports Illustrated,* June 17, 2002: p. 36.

Taylor, Phil. "He's Back." *Sports Illustrated,* December 25, 1995: p. 22.

WEB SITES

http://sportsillustrated.cnn.com/basketball

This section of the official Web site for Sports Illustrated *magazine provides full coverage of the NBA, with the latest info on the league, news articles, and player pages.*

http://www.shaq.com

Shaq's official site has tons of info on his professional achievements on and off the court along with current basketball season news, interactive games, and video clips.

www.nba.com/lakers

This site features bios, stats, and up-to-date information on Shaquille's games with the Lakers.

FILMOGRAPHY

Platinum Comedy Series: Roasting Shaquille O'Neal (2002)
Alex Thomas: Straight Clownin' (2002)
The Wash (2001)
Shaq's MVP Comedy Roast (2001)
MTV Icon: Janet Jackson (2001)
Official 2000 NBA Championship Video: Los Angeles Lakers (2000)
NBA Now! Showmen of Today (2000)
NBA Live 2001: The Music Videos (2000)
The Story of Fathers & Sons (1999)
He Got Game (1998)
Breaking Out—The Alcatraz Concert Live! (1998)
NBA in the Paint (1997)
NBA Courtside Comedy (1997)
Steel (1997)
Shaq 'Round the World (1997)
NBA Grooves (1997)
I Am Your Child (1997)
Good Burger (1997)
Broken Record (1997)
Special Effects: Anything Can Happen (1996)
NBA Furious Finishes (1996)
Kazaam (1996)
WCW—Bash at the Beach—Hulk Hogan vs. Ric Flair (1994)
Shaquille O'Neal: Shaq Diesel—The Music Videos (1994)
Shaquille O'Neal—Larger Than Life (1994)
NBA Super Slams 2 (1994)
Blue Chips (1994)
CB4 (1993)
Shaq Attack—In Your Face: On and Off the Court (1992)

DISCOGRAPHY

Respect (1998)

The Best of Shaquille O'Neal (1996)

You Can't Stop the Reign (1996)

Shaq Fu: Da Return (1994)

Shaq Diesel (1993)

INDEX